· A ·
SEPARATE
BATTLE

Women and the Civil War

Thousands of northern women went south to teach the freed slaves during and after the Civil War.

· A ·
SEPARATE
BATTLE

Women and the Civil War

·

INA CHANG

SCHOLASTIC INC.
New York Toronto London Auckland Sydney

ISBN 0-590-46840-5

12 11 10 9 8 7 6 5 4 3 2 1   4 5 6 7 8 9/9

Printed in the U.S.A.   34

First Scholastic printing, March 1994

for my grandmother

Contents

The Grimké family lived in this prosperous neighborhood on Charleston's waterfront. This scene was painted in 1831, not long after Angelina Grimké left for the North.

Voices for Freedom

Angelina Grimké grew up in Charleston, South Carolina, in the early 1800s, a wealthy and privileged daughter of the South. Her family lived in an elegant three-story townhouse on Church Street, overlooking the bustling harbor where tall-masted schooners unloaded their cargoes: furniture and machinery from the North, rum and sugar from the West Indies, and fine cloth and silverware from England. The Grimké mansion was a center of Charleston social life, the site of fashionable tea parties and formal dinners. Like most upper-class children, Angelina and her brothers and sisters studied French and Latin and took piano lessons.

One day in school, thirteen-year-old Angelina watched as a young black boy—a slave who belonged to the schoolmistress—was ordered to come in and open a window. The boy's head had been shaved, and he could barely drag himself across the room. When he turned around, it was obvious why he was so crippled: His back and legs bore the marks of a recent whipping, and the wounds were still encrusted with blood. Angelina was so horrified that she collapsed to the floor. "He had been so dreadfully whipped that he could hardly walk," she recalled years later. "So horrible was the impression produced upon my mind by his heartbroken countenance and crippled person that I fainted away."

Blacks had been enslaved in the South for nearly two hundred years by the time Angelina was born. One out of every three Southerners was a slave. Owning slaves was a symbol of success, and the Grimkés were among the most successful in Charleston society. The cooks, butlers, nursemaids, stable boys, and washer-women at the mansion were all slaves, as were the black men, women, and children who worked in the fields at the family plantation two hundred miles from Charleston.

What Angelina had seen in the schoolhouse was not so unusual. One of her neighbors flogged her slaves daily, and the woman's raving insults could be heard up and down the street. Another neighbor family beat their slaves so severely that they had to borrow servants whenever they had company, so that the guests wouldn't see the unsightly wounds. Even Angelina's older brother Henry boasted that he would be sore for several days after whipping a slave.

By the time she was twenty-four, when other young southern women were looking for husbands and preparing to become mistresses of their own slaveowning households, Grimké had decided to leave the South. She was convinced that slavery was a sin, and she could no longer stand to live among slaveholders. She moved to Philadelphia and joined the small but growing antislavery movement in the North.

By this time, slavery had been abolished in the northern states, but Grimké discovered that few Northerners cared about the plight of slaves in the South; in fact, many were frightened by the idea of millions of blacks being freed. As Grimké traveled from town to town speaking out against slavery, she was heckled, pelted with apples, and often locked out of churches where she was scheduled to speak. Still, she was convinced that she could change people's minds: "I am confident not many years will roll over before the horrible traffic in human beings will be destroyed in this land. . . ." she wrote in her diary in 1834.

Grimké and other women who joined the abolitionist movement in the decades before the Civil War faced opposition from many sides. Not only was their cause unpopular, but the women

Angelina Grimké lived a very different kind of life after she left Charleston. This portrait shows her in the plain dress she adopted once she went north.

were called indecent and unladylike for expressing their views in public.

Among the women abolitionists, few were as bold as Sojourner Truth, a former slave. Tall and muscular, with a commanding voice and a lightning wit, Truth was at her best before an unfriendly crowd. At a women's rights rally in Akron, Ohio, in 1851, the first women to speak were constantly interrupted by men who insisted that females were inferior. A crowd of boys jeered from the balcony. When Sojourner Truth rose from her seat, and the unruly members of the audience saw that a six-foot-tall black woman was approaching the stage, they hissed loudly.

Although she never learned to read or write, Sojourner Truth was one of the most brilliant communicators in the antislavery movement. "She would wring our hearts," said a fellow abolitionist, "and wreathe our faces with smiles, and even convulse us with laughter, at her story of old slave life. . . ."

Standing at the podium, Truth fixed her gaze on one of the men who had interrupted the meeting. "That man over there," she said in a strong voice, "says that women need to be helped into carriages, and lifted over ditches, and to have the best place everywhere. Nobody ever helped *me* into carriages, or over mud puddles, or gave me any best place. And aren't I a woman?" She pushed the sleeve of her gray dress up to her shoulder. "Look at me! Look at my arm! I have plowed and planted, and gathered into barns, and no man could head me. And aren't I a woman? I could work as much and eat as much as a man—when I could get it—and bear the lash as well. And aren't I a woman?" By now, her voice was thundering through the hall. "I have borne thirteen children and seen them most all sold off into slavery, and when I cried out with a mother's grief, none but Jesus heard. *And aren't I a woman?*" When Truth was finished, the audience erupted into loud cheers.

Sojourner Truth and other women charged the antislavery movement with emotion. They told about slave families being torn apart, and slave mothers brutally restrained as their children were sold away. They asked the white women of the North to imagine how they would feel if the same thing happened to their own families. Angelina Grimké even wrote a pamphlet for southern women, in which she asked, "I appeal to you, my friends, as mothers; Are you willing to enslave *your* children?" But her pleas only made white Southerners more angry. The pamphlet was publicly burned in Charleston, and the mayor warned Grimké's family that if she returned home to visit, she would be arrested and thrown into prison.

But of all the northern women opposed to slavery, none made a greater impact with her words than Harriet Beecher Stowe, a writer from a prominent New England family of preachers and educators. While Sojourner Truth was delivering lectures and other antislavery women were organizing rallies and circulating petitions, forty-year-old Stowe was in Maine writing a story about slavery called *Uncle Tom's Cabin.*

It began as a weekly series in 1851 in an antislavery newspaper published in Washington, D.C., called *The National Era.* At first, Stowe planned to write no more than three or four episodes. But

One of the cruelest aspects of slavery was the separation of slave parents and children. Here, a slave woman and her daughter cling to each other on the auction block.

Harriet Beecher Stowe, the author of *Uncle Tom's Cabin*, said that she began to understand the suffering of slave mothers when her own infant son died of cholera in 1849.

readers demanded more of the dramatic tale. What would become of Uncle Tom, the gentle, saintly slave who was sold to the evil plantation owner Simon Legree? And what was the future of the beautiful slave woman Eliza, who fled to freedom by leaping from ice floe to ice floe across the half-frozen Ohio River with her child in her arms? Fan letters poured into the newspaper's offices, and by the time the last of forty-five episodes appeared ten months

Uncle Tom's Cabin **attracted international attention to the American antislavery movement.**

later, Stowe had moved thousands of readers to tears over the cruelty of the slave system.

Stowe's story was published in book form in 1852. *Uncle Tom's Cabin* became an instant bestseller, generating antislavery sentiment throughout the North. People who had never visited the South or paid attention to the abolitionists were outraged by the horrors of slavery that Stowe described. Within two months, three hundred thousand copies of the novel had been sold. The publisher ran three printing presses twenty-four hours a day to meet the demand. Within a year, more than a million copies had been sold in the United States and England, and the book was soon translated into French, German, Italian, Portuguese, and half a dozen other languages.

Uncle Tom's Cabin was written at a time when the country was already bitterly divided over slavery. But the dispute was not merely about whether slavery was right or wrong. Slavery was the centerpiece in a larger struggle as the country expanded westward. As new states—including Missouri, Texas, Kansas, and

♦ Uncle Tom in the South ♦

In the South, Harriet Beecher Stowe's antislavery book *Uncle Tom's Cabin* was treated like poison and branded a "filthy negro novel." Southerners were furious that Stowe dared to attack the southern way of life when she had never lived in a slave state and had almost no firsthand knowledge of slavery. The *Southern Literary Messenger* called the book "dangerous and dirty"; a reviewer for the *Alabama Planter* wrote, "The woman who wrote it must be either a very bad or a very fanatical person." One Tennessee clergyman made an even more personal attack, calling Stowe "as ugly as Original sin."

As Stowe's novel grew more popular in the North, inspiring Uncle Tom plays, souvenirs, and songs, Southerners unleashed a counterattack, producing a crop of "anti-Tom" novels describing healthy slaves cared for by kind owners. Many, such as *Uncle Robin in His Cabin in Virginia and Tom Without One in Boston*, pointed out that blacks in the North often made starvation wages and lived in worse housing than the slaves.

Stowe could have ignored the criticism, but instead she proceeded to write *A Key to Uncle Tom's Cabin*, a book of anecdotes, stories, and documents that supported her depiction of slavery in *Uncle Tom's Cabin*.

CANADA

MINNESOTA

WISCONSIN

Flint●

MICHIGAN

Dubuque●

IOWA

Chicago●

ILLINOIS

INDIANA

OHIO

Cleveland●

Akron●

Pittsburgh●

NEW
YORK

Rochester●

Syracuse●
Auburn●

PENNSYLVANIA

Philadelphia●

Gettysburg●

MAINE

Concord●

Boston●

VERMONT

NEW
HAMPSHIRE

MASS.

RHODE ISLAND
CONNECTICUT

New
York●

NEW JERSEY

St. Louis●

MISSOURI

Cairo●

KENTUCKY

Antietam●

Washington, D.C.✪

Manassas●

Fredericksburg●

Richmond●

VIRGINIA

Appomattox● Petersburg●

Baltimore●

Annapolis●

DELAWARE

MARYLAND

Atlantic Ocean

Raleigh●

NORTH CAROLINA

ARKANSAS

TENNESSEE

Shiloh●

Chattanooga●

SOUTH CAROLINA

Columbia●

Charleston●

Atlanta●

MISSISSIPPI

ALABAMA

Macon●

Beaufort●

Savannah●

GEORGIA

LOUISIANA

Vicksburg●

TEXAS

Mobile●

Baton Rouge●

New Orleans●

FLORIDA

Gulf of Mexico

NSAS
ERR.

The War Begins
April 12, 1861

Free States

Slave States

Confederate States

Territories or
Unorganized

By the time the Civil War began,
seven of the thirty-three states had
broken away from the Union and
formed the Confederate States of
America. Within weeks, Virginia,
North Carolina, Tennessee and
Arkansas joined them. The re-
maining slave states of Delaware,
Maryland, Kentucky and Missouri
remained torn between the two
sides but never left the Union.

© 1991 Laing Communications Inc.

Nebraska—entered the Union, the North and South argued over whether it would be a slave or free state. Neither side wanted the other to control the destiny of the nation.

The growing antislavery mood in the North angered Southerners who were already disturbed at how much money the North was making from shipping and processing southern cotton bought

---

♦ Harriet Tubman ♦

Harriet Tubman was born on a Maryland plantation and worked as a field slave until she escaped to the North in 1849. At the time of her escape, she was about thirty years old. A tough, fearless woman who stood only five feet tall, Tubman felt it was her mission to return to the slave states and lead her people to freedom. She made nineteen trips, mostly to Maryland and Delaware, to lead runaways northward. The slaves in the area called her "Moses," after Moses of the Bible, who led his people out of slavery and to the Promised Land.

Tubman usually made her trips during the winter, when the nights were long, and she led slaves in the darkness along backroads and through the woods. During the day, she hid them in barns, potato holes, swamps, and in the homes of antislavery people who were part of a secret network called the "Underground Railroad."

A brilliant planner, Tubman carried forged passes to fool patrolmen on the lookout for runaways, and she paid local blacks to take down fugitive posters. She also used disguises. Once, when she had to travel through a town where one of her former masters lived, she dressed as an old woman and shuffled down the street carrying several live chickens tied with a string. When she turned a corner and saw her old master walking toward her, she quickly released the string, and as the chickens flew off in a squawking cloud of feathers, she ran after them. Her former master never saw her face.

Tubman became friends with many leading abolitionists in the North. A number of them allowed her to hide fugitive slaves in their homes along the escape route to Canada, where runaways were safe from slave catchers. She also became an antislavery speaker,

at low prices. They felt that Northerners were fighting the spread of slavery in order to gain more power, and that people such as Angelina Grimké, Sojourner Truth, and Harriet Beecher Stowe were purposely painting a distorted picture of southern life.

Most southern whites actually owned no slaves; only one out of four families had black servants. But because slaveowning was

Harriet Tubman's successful rescue efforts angered slave-holders, who once offered $40,000 for her capture.

lecturing on her experiences in slavery and her dangerous rescue missions. Tubman liked to tell the story of one trip in which she and twenty-five runaways hid in a swamp all day and night. One of the men lost his nerve and decided to turn back. Unwilling to let him endanger the others, Tubman pulled out a revolver and pointed it at his head. "Move or die!" she told him. He kept going, and a few days later was a free man.

During the war, Tubman worked as a nurse and a scout for the Union Army. Afterward, she settled in Auburn, New York, with her elderly parents, who she had rescued from Maryland years before. With help from abolitionist friends, she opened a home for elderly blacks in Auburn and continued to give speeches. At a women's rights meeting in Rochester, New York, in the 1880s, she told her audience, "Yes, ladies, I was the conductor of the Underground Railroad for eight years, and I can say what most conductors can't say—I never ran my train off the track, and I never lost a passenger."

the path to wealth and status in the South, most whites defended slavery as a cornerstone of southern life and southern values.

Letitia Burwell, who was raised on a Virginia plantation, believed that her family's slaves were happy with their lives. "All were merry-hearted, and among them I never saw a discontented face," she wrote. Burwell could not even imagine slaveowners treating their slaves unkindly. "What man would pay a thousand dollars for a piece of property, and fail to take the best possible care of it?" she said.

Mary Chesnut, who came from one of the wealthiest slaveowning families in South Carolina, felt guilty about certain aspects of slavery. "God forgive us," she wrote in her diary, "but ours is a *monstrous* system. . . . Perhaps the rest of the world is as bad." Still, Chesnut felt that most slaves were "hard, unpleasant, unromantic, undeveloped savage Africans"—not the sympathetic blacks portrayed in *Uncle Tom's Cabin*.

By 1861, just nine years after *Uncle Tom's Cabin* was published, the country could no longer hold together. Eleven slave states, feeling that northern opposition to slavery threatened their entire way of life, broke away from the Union and formed a separate country, the Confederate States of America. On April 12, the Confederates fired on a fort full of Federal soldiers in Charleston Harbor, in full view of the mansion where Angelina Grimké had been raised. The Civil War had begun.

Across the North, men and boys eager to prove their patriotism and force the rebel states back into the Union answered President Abraham Lincoln's call for volunteer soldiers. Whole families flocked to recruitment rallies, where local enlistees showed off their new uniforms and army captains delivered stirring speeches. Many women pushed their husbands and sons to enlist and take part in the noble fight. At a rally in Wisconsin, one woman stood up and declared that if she had another husband, she would make him sign up as well.

Southern patriotism was equally as strong. In Richmond, Virginia, the Confederate capital, regiments marched and drilled through the streets while townspeople cheered. "The town is crowded with soldiers," Mary Chesnut wrote in her diary. "These new ones are running in. . . . They fear the war will be over

Citizens of Charleston watch from their rooftops as the Confederates fire on Fort Sumter in Charleston Harbor. No one was killed in that first battle of the Civil War.

before they get a sight of the fun. Every man from every little country precinct wants a place in the picture."

But the glory, parades, and excitement quickly gave way to fear and sadness. Although few people expected the conflict to last past the end of summer, many women were filled with dread as they watched their family members march off to war. "Everybody was on the streets to see the troops go off," said a Virginia woman whose husband joined the Confederate Army, "and I took my stand with the others and watched as the cavalry rode past us. We kept our handkerchiefs waving all the time our friends were riding by, and when we saw our husbands and brothers we tried to cheer, but our voices were husky. The last thing I saw of my husband he was wringing the hand of an old friend who was not going, tears were streaming down his cheeks and he was saying, 'For God's sake, take care of my wife.'"

Harriet Beecher Stowe was one of the first prominent Northerners to declare her support for the Union's call to arms. "This is a cause to die for," she wrote in *The National Era*, "and—thanks be to God!—our young men embrace it . . . and are ready to die." Even so, when her twenty-one-year-old son, Fred, announced that he was quitting Harvard Medical School to enlist, she tried to stop him. She urged him to finish his studies, then enlist as an army surgeon. For days she pleaded with him, even bringing him to the dean of the medical school for a stern lecture. But Fred wouldn't listen. Finally, in the middle of a heated argument, he told her bluntly why he had to join up: He could never stand to hear people say, "Harriet Beecher Stowe's son is a coward." The next day, he signed up for Company A of the First Massachusetts Volunteer Infantry.

Several weeks later Stowe saw her son briefly when his regiment stopped in New Jersey on its way south. "Fred was overjoyed," Stowe wrote to her husband. "He was in high spirits, in spite of the weight of blue overcoat, knapsack, etc., etc., that he would formerly have declared intolerable for half an hour." After a brief visit, she filled Fred's bag with oranges, then left town. "So our boys come to manhood in a day," she wrote. "Now I am watching anxiously for the evening paper to tell me that the regiment has reached Washington in safety." ◆

Troops were sent off with great fanfare at the start of the war. Here, a crowd gathers in Detroit to watch the First Michigan Volunteer Infantry receive its flags.

Women frequently gathered in groups to make clothing for the troops. Sewing circles provided a chance to socialize and exchange news of the war. This illustration, like most drawings in newspapers and magazines of the day, shows a romanticized view of women. Women were portrayed as delicate and demure, even though their work required determination and energy.

♦ T W O ♦

Supplying the Armies

As troops in both the North and South drilled endlessly, waiting for the action to begin, thousands of women were busy outfitting volunteers for the army. Each soldier would need a uniform, as well as bedding, socks, and whatever few comforts of home he could carry on his back. Women went to work at a frenzied rate weaving, cutting, and sewing. Whole companies were completely outfitted by local women, with everything from clothing to tents to battle flags.

Neither the troops nor those at home realized what camp life would be like. Women were sending soldiers off with such impractical items as down pillows and fancy quilts with lines of poetry lovingly embroidered on them. Encouraged by men who wanted to look dashing as they departed for war, the women created a hodgepodge of ornate "uniforms." In New Orleans, brightly colored fabrics and loud patterns were preferred. One woman described the outfits as "the most bewildering combination of brilliant, intense reds, greens, yellows, and blues in big flowers." A Louisiana company was fitted out in baggy scarlet trousers with wide blue sashes, blue shirts, and jackets trimmed with lace. Northern soldiers were sent off in equally showy costumes, some featuring broad-brimmed hats with feathers and baggy pantaloons.

Among the items that women made in a wide array of colors was a cotton headdress called a havelock. Invented by a British general stationed in India, the havelock was a cap with a piece of cloth that hung down in back and shaded the neck. A northern newspaper had suggested that havelocks were just the thing to protect Union soldiers from the unfamiliar, glaring heat of the southern sun.

"Havelocks were turned out by the thousands," one woman recalled, "of all patterns and sizes, and of every conceivable material." But when a group of northern women visited the Nineteenth Illinois Regiment in camp, they found the havelocks being used as bandages, nightcaps, and everything but what they were intended for. The word went out, and havelock production stopped just as suddenly as it had begun.

Women learned from their errors, and in time they were producing supplies with factory-like efficiency. "The amount of *work* we have accomplished is a wonder to ourselves, to say nothing of the world," a South Carolina woman remarked in 1861. Church groups and casual sewing circles were transformed into soldiers' aid societies. Foot-treadle sewing machines, invented in 1849, were in great demand, and women pooled their money to buy them. Production increased dramatically: A shirt that took two days to sew by hand took only about an hour by machine.

Women brought their knitting everywhere. "I do not know when I have seen a woman without knitting in her hand," said Mary Chesnut of South Carolina, whose husband was a Confederate officer. "'Socks for the soldiers' is the cry. . . . It gives a quaint look, the twinkling of needles, and the everlasting sock dangling."

As the shirts and blankets piled up, it was not always clear where they should be sent. Neither army had an organized supply system, so packages were often delivered to the wrong place, or arrived after the troops had moved on.

Dr. Elizabeth Blackwell of New York, the first woman in the United States to earn a medical degree, realized early on that the Union Army needed a system for distributing its supplies. She organized thousands of women in New York City in April 1861 into a volunteer organization called the Women's Central Asso-

A southern woman fits a Confederate soldier with a linen havelock. This type of headgear was popular on both sides early in the war.

ciation of Relief, or WCAR. They planned to collect and distribute donations of all kinds from citizens, including medical supplies, and they set up a training course for nurses, taught by Dr. Blackwell.

But the WCAR had no official status, and people soon began pressuring Union leaders to create an official organization to handle

Members of the Soldiers' Aid Society of Springfield, Illinois, pose with food and clothing they have prepared for the Union troops.

supplies and manage army hospitals. The U.S. Army Medical
Bureau certainly wasn't up to the job; at the start of the war, the
bureau employed only twenty-eight surgeons, had no general
hospital, and lacked a system for collecting or transporting supplies.

In July 1861, the Union government established the U.S. Sanitary Commission. The WCAR became a major branch of the
commission, and soon seven thousand local soldiers' aid societies
joined the network. Headed by men but staffed mainly by women
volunteers, the commission took charge of setting up supply stations and hospitals, hiring nurses, and collecting donations. It sent
inspectors to Union hospitals and taught troops in camp how to
cook their food properly and prevent the spread of disease.

Commission volunteers sorted and mailed donations and made
sure people knew what supplies were needed. They also educated

**The Sanitary Commission sent representatives to army camps and battle-
fields. Here, a group of men and women stands by a Sanitary Commission outpost near Alexandria, Virginia.**

citizens about what not to send. At the outset of the war, women had sent butter, pies, crates of fresh eggs, and even fried chicken to the commission offices. After traveling hundreds or sometimes thousands of miles, much of the food rotted. "Baggage cars were soon flooded with fermenting sweetmeats, and broken pots of jelly, that ought never to have been sent," said one Sanitary Commission volunteer. "Decaying fruit and vegetables, pastry and cake in a

♦ Clara Barton ♦

Clara Barton was a genius at organization, and the Civil War provided her with endless opportunities to use her skills. She had no official connection to the military, but she became so involved in collecting and delivering supplies to northern troops around Washington, D.C., that she referred to the Union's Army of the Potomac as "my own army."

Barton chose an unusual path for a woman. She became a teacher at age fifteen, opened her own school when she was in her twenties, and was the first woman ever hired for a government job in Washington, D.C. She never married. She was forty years old and worked as a clerk in the government patent office when the war began.

Two weeks into the war, a regiment from Barton's home state of Massachusetts was attacked by a proslavery mob in Baltimore on the way to the capital. Three men were killed, and others were badly injured. When Barton learned that some of the soldiers were her former students, she rushed to the train

Clara Barton often showed up at camps and battlefields with desperately needed provisions long before Sanitary Commission workers arrived.

demoralized condition, badly canned meats and soups . . . were necessarily thrown away *en route*."

By the second year of the war, aid societies had a better idea of what the soldiers needed. Women who had put their money and effort into making havelocks now concentrated on such items as mosquito netting. When army doctors asked for supplies for dressing wounds, women quickly formed "lint and bandage asso-

station to meet them. She found the men dazed and bleeding, and missing most of their belongings.

The sight drove Barton to immediate action. Because the army had no supplies for the men and no place for them to camp, they were taken to the Senate Chamber at the Capitol and left to fend for themselves. Barton enlisted the help of a few other women and brought the soldiers all the provisions she could find. "We . . . emptied our pockets and came home to tear up old sheets for towels and handkerchiefs," she told a friend, "and have filled a large box with all manner of serving utensils, thread, needles, thimbles, scissors, pins, buttons, strings, salves, tallow, etc. etc." She fed them, bandaged their wounds, and read aloud from a newspaper while sitting at the vice president's desk.

By the time the regiment left Washington a few weeks later, news of Barton's efforts had reached the soldiers' families and local aid societies, and they began sending her supplies. Convinced that she was better organized than any government department, Barton also took out newspaper advertisements asking for money and provisions. She loaded the supplies into wagons and took them straight to the camps and battlefields around Washington.

In time, Barton had three warehouses full of provisions and was using four large wagons borrowed from the army. She eventually quit her job at the patent office and ran her supply operation full time until the end of the war.

Barton did not abandon relief work when the war ended, however. She became involved in the Red Cross, an international agency devoted to disaster relief and wartime medical assistance. She founded a branch of the Red Cross in the United States in 1881 and devoted the rest of her life to the organization.

ciations." The bandages were simple strips of cloth, rolled and fastened. Lint, used to dress wounds, was gathered by turning a plate bottom-side-up, laying a piece of cloth over it, and scraping the cloth with a knife. Old tablecloths, sheets, and even rags were turned into piles of lint. At the time, doctors believed that keeping the lint wet helped wounds heal faster, and many nurses spent long hours going from bed to bed, moistening wounds with a sponge dipped in a basin of water.

The Chicago office of the Sanitary Commission was one of the largest branches, and it received mountains of donations from several states. Curious to see what was coming in, a volunteer named Mary Livermore went into the packing room one day to poke through the newly arrived boxes. She found a neat assortment of handmade socks, shirts, trousers, and edible treats. One package held a dressing gown with one pocket filled with hickory nuts and another stuffed with ginger snaps. Nearly every parcel contained a personal note, wishing the soldiers well or asking them to write. One woman enclosed a note that read, "These cookies are expressly for the sick soldiers, and if anybody else eats them, *I hope they will choke him!*"

By 1863, the Chicago branch had sent thirty thousand boxes of supplies to army camps and hospitals. But the cost of transporting the supplies had nearly depleted its treasury. Somehow, the volunteers needed to raise more money. Mary Livermore and her friend Jane Hoge devised an ambitious plan: They would collect donations of goods from citizens throughout the region and sell the items at a huge fair.

When the women said that the fair could raise $25,000, commission officials laughed at them. They went ahead with the project anyway. With the help of other women volunteers, they placed notices in newspapers in several states, asking for goods and money. The women wrote to governors, ministers, and teachers, telling them to spread the word. They mailed out twenty thousand flyers with instructions on how to send contributions. Within a few months, major cities were holding "fair meetings" to collect pledges and donations for the Chicago fair. Throughout the North people rifled through attics and closets for long-forgotten treasures to donate. Everything from silverware to pianos, horses, and even

Mary Livermore of the Chicago Sanitary Commission

barrels of cologne arrived at the fair offices. A fifty-year-old free black woman who had nine children still enslaved in the South sent a handmade sheet. Another ex-slave gave a pair of socks that she had made for her teenage son, who died fighting for the Union Army. Michigan farmers donated crates of fruit, and the women of Dubuque, Iowa, sent hundreds of cooked ducks, chickens, and turkeys.

The fair opened on the morning of October 27, 1863, with a spectacular parade. After two and a half years of war, the people of Chicago needed a celebration to lift their spirits. By the time the procession began at ten o'clock, eager spectators lined the streets. A military band kicked off the parade with a long drum roll, and soon patriotic music was blaring all along the three-mile route. Flags flew from rooftops and church steeples. When a line of carriages rolled by filled with wounded soldiers from nearby army hospitals, the crowd gave a great roar and showered the men with flowers. A wagon displaying captured Confederate flags drew thundering cheers all along the parade route.

At noon, the six huge fair buildings were opened. Flags were draped everywhere, and band music echoed from building to building. The halls became so crowded that ticket sales had to be stopped repeatedly. The dining hall, which fed three hundred people at a time, was packed all day long, and dozens of performers entertained the fairgoers. Outside, thoroughbred colts and oxen were auctioned off.

The fair was a stunning success. The Chicago Sanitary Commission had raised close to $100,000. Before long, "sanitary fairs" were being organized in New York, Cleveland, Boston, Pittsburgh, St. Louis, and dozens of other cities, each fair more elaborate than the last.

The 1864 Philadelphia fair was perhaps the most ambitious. The organizers formed dozens of committees, each responsible for collecting a certain kind of donation to sell. There was a Committee on Umbrellas, Parasols, and Canes, and a Committee on Trimmings, Ribbons, Laces, and Embroideries. Even artificial teeth and dental instruments had their own committee. The Miscellaneous Committee was a huge success, collecting hoop skirts and corsets, soap and candles, billiard tables, and artificial arms and legs.

The main hall of the New York fair of April 1864, which raised more than two million dollars

The South had no Sanitary Commission, and women of the Confederacy organized on a much smaller scale. They took turns meeting troops at train stations with hot meals, even as their own pantries dwindled, and they delivered hospital supplies in their own wagons. Women donated their brass goods to the army to be melted down and made into weapons.

The success of the Sanitary Commission fair in Chicago in 1863 led to dozens of similar fairs across the North. This illustration shows the main building of the second Chicago fair, held in 1865.

In Charleston, in the spring of 1862, the Ladies Gunboat Fair sold four thousand raffle tickets for a chance to win silverware, watches, and a diamond ring. In Columbia, a group of young women set up a refreshment area at the train station for sick and wounded soldiers waiting for connecting trains. Before long, the women were also providing each soldier with a bath, a change of

clothes, and a cot to sleep on. They served as many as three hundred men in one day.

The Confederate government depended even more than the North on contributions from its plantations, farms, and homes. "The supply of money, clothing and hospital stores derived from this generous source is not only of immense value in itself," said one government official, "but the most cheering indication of the spirit of our people." ◆

Louisa May Alcott wrote a book about her experiences as an army nurse, which launched her into a successful writing career. Alcott's best-known novel was *Little Women*, the story of four northern sisters during the Civil War.

♦ T H R E E ♦

Hospital Duty

I never began the year in a stranger place than this," Louisa May Alcott wrote in her diary in January 1863. "Five hundred miles from home, alone among strangers, doing painful duties all day long, & leading a life of constant excitement. . . ." Compared with Alcott's quiet hometown of Concord, Massachusetts, the nation's capital seemed like a huge carnival. More than a quarter million soldiers were camped in and around Washington, D.C.; the bright lights, the rumble of carriages, and the constant thunder of marching feet made the war seem real to her for the first time.

Alcott was a volunteer nurse at the Union Hotel Hospital, a musty old hotel that had been converted into an army medical facility. On her third day there, a flood of wounded soldiers arrived from the Battle of Fredericksburg in nearby Virginia. Alcott was startled awake that morning by shouts of "They've come! They've come!" By the time she was out of bed and dressed, forty horsedrawn ambulances were waiting outside the hospital door, loaded with ragged, bleeding men.

Alcott had looked forward to the arrival of the wounded, but when the gruesome cargo was unloaded, she felt a rush of panic and suddenly wished she were safe at home in Concord. She managed to push aside her fears. "The sight of several stretchers, each with its legless, armless, or desperately wounded occupant, entering my ward, admonished me that I was there to work, not to wonder or weep," she later recalled. "So I corked up my feelings, and returned to the path of duty. . . ."

Alcott's job was to oversee a ward with forty beds in what had been the hotel ballroom. Her patients included not only the wounded from Fredericksburg, but also soldiers from nearby camps with pneumonia, dysentery, typhoid fever, measles, and other diseases. She spent her days "washing faces, serving rations, giving medicine, and sitting in a very hard chair." She read newspapers to the men and helped them write letters to their families. In the evenings she passed out more medicine, wiped feverish faces, sang lullabies, and moistened the dressings on the soldiers' wounds.

As the days passed, Alcott discovered that the job of army nurse was far more than treating sickness and cleaning wounds. She sat for days by the bed of a New Jersey boy who had only a slight wound but was haunted by memories of the Battle of Fredericksburg. In his mind, the battle was still raging. "He lay cheering his comrades on, hurrying them back, then counting them as they fell around him," Alcott said. Sometimes he would grab her by the arm as if to pull her out of the way of a bursting shell. Again and again, she relived the scene with him.

One day she went to her room for a moment's rest only to find a young woman sitting on her bed, looking dazed and miserable. The woman was the sister of a soldier who had died during the night. Not knowing what else to do, Alcott put her arms around the woman "and began to cry in a very helpless but hearty way." The woman immediately joined in. "It so happened I could not have done a better thing," Alcott wrote, "for, though not a word was spoken, each felt the other's sympathy; and, in the silence, our handkerchiefs were more eloquent than words."

More than three thousand women served as nurses during the Civil War. It was a new profession for women; the hospital was still a man's world. Before the war, almost all nurses in army hospitals were men, usually recovering soldiers who felt well enough to move about. These helpers were untrained and often

Nurses and patients gathered at the Armory Square General Hospital in Washington, D.C. The ward was decorated for a holiday, probably the Fourth of July.

too feeble to be of much use at all. With a war raging, better nurses were needed, and scores of women answered the challenge. Much like Louisa May Alcott, they sought the excitement of war. For many, being a nurse was the next best thing to joining the army. When Alcott found out that she had been hired as a nurse, she rushed home and declared to her family, "I've enlisted!"

The Union Army recognized the need for women nurses sooner

than the Confederates did. Just a few months after the war began, the U.S. government appointed a superintendent of women nurses to screen volunteers and establish the rules for hospital duty. Dorothea Dix, a stern-faced fifty-nine-year-old woman who dressed only in brown or black, was chosen for the job. Dix set up strict requirements for joining the nursing corps. Volunteers had to be "plain in appearance" and at least thirty years old. Applicants wearing hoop skirts, the popular fashion of the day, were rejected. Jewelry was also unacceptable. Scores of would-be nurses were turned away because Dix was determined to weed out anyone with romantic notions about hospital work.

In the South, the taboo against women joining the medical profession was even stronger because females were considered much too delicate for such work. As a result, the Confederacy had far fewer women nurses than the Union did. But a number of

♦ Dorothea Dix ♦

"She is a kind soul but very queer & arbitrary," one nurse wrote of Dorothea Dix. Others were not so generous when describing the Union Army's superintendent of women nurses. One nurse nicknamed her "Dragon Dix" and another called her "a self-sealing can of horror tied up in red tape."

Dix's job would have been difficult even for someone with a more agreeable personality. She was responsible for screening thousands of nursing applicants, and she had to work with officials and surgeons who resented her authority. Even though her requirements for joining the nursing corps were rigid and she may have rejected very able women simply because they looked too stylish, she succeeded in sending out a clear message: Nursing was serious work.

A somber woman who stood straight as a rod and wore her dark brown hair in a neat coil, Dix made a name for herself before the war as a reformer of mental hospitals. She spent years investigating the treatment of the mentally ill in the United States and England, and ran a one-woman campaign to improve conditions in insane asylums and pressure the U.S. government to set up more

women took the initiative, becoming unofficial nurses and hospital helpers. Sally Tompkins of Richmond established her own twenty-two-bed hospital in a friend's home, and the facility earned such a glowing reputation that Jefferson Davis, the president of the Confederacy, awarded her the rank of captain. Other southern women volunteered as nurses when the fighting came near their homes, and many offered their homes as temporary hospitals.

In both the North and South, army hospitals were set up in a hurry and were often overcrowded and unsanitary. The Union Hotel Hospital, even though it was in the nation's capital, was among the worst—"cold, damp, dirty, full of vile odors from wounds, kitchens, wash rooms, stables," according to Louisa May Alcott. The drafty, three-story structure had dark, narrow passages, damp cellars, and rotting woodwork. Disease spread quickly among the patients and the hospital staff.

humane state institutions.

Dix's nurses respected her accomplishments, but were frustrated by her sour manner and lack of managerial ability. Nurses complained that she played favorites, and spent too much time making surprise inspections of hospitals and checking on supplies. Dix herself was disappointed with her wartime experience and considered it only a minor episode in her career. "This is not the work I would have my life judged by," she said. After the war, she returned to her work with the mentally ill.

Dorothea Dix, the Union Army's superintendent of women nurses

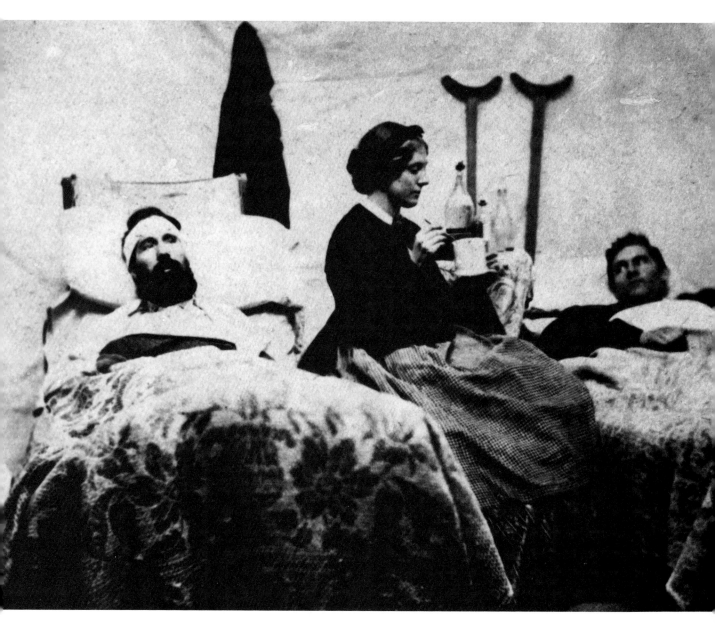

A nurse tends to two wounded soldiers at a Union hospital in Tennessee.

Six weeks after she arrived at the hospital, Alcott became ill. "My head felt like a cannon ball," she later wrote. "My feet had a tendency to cleave to the floor; the walls at times undulated in a most disagreeable manner; people looked unnaturally big. . . ." She had typhoid fever. At about the same time, the matron—or head nurse—of the hospital, Hannah Ropes, died of the same disease. Alcott was sent home to Concord, where she recovered from the illness but never fully regained her strength.

Conditions were even worse in field hospitals. Set up to treat soldiers as close to the battlefield as possible, a field hospital was often nothing more than a cluster of tents or an abandoned building with a few tables and cots set up inside. Supplies and medicines were frequently in short supply, and getting clean water often involved a long hike. After the Battle of Gettysburg, in July 1863, Sophronia Bucklin of New York went to work at the main Union field hospital, which had been set up where part of the bloody, three-day conflict took place. About twenty-three thousand Union men were killed or wounded at Gettysburg, and the Confederates suffered even more casualties. When Bucklin arrived at the town, she found a sickening scene. "It seemed impossible to tread the streets without walking over maimed men," she later wrote. "They lay like trees uprooted by a tornado. . . ." Everywhere the grass was stained with blood, and dead horses lay in heaps.

The Union field hospital at Gettysburg was made up of five hundred white canvas tents, lined up in neat rows. Surgeons worked night and day cutting off shattered limbs, and nurses "washed faces, combed out matted hair, bandaged slight wounds, and administered drinks of raspberry vinegar and lemon syrup," according to Bucklin. When heavy rains fell, the doctors and nurses had to wade through thick mud to tend to the men. More than once, Bucklin had to fish her shoes out of the muddy water with an umbrella handle before getting dressed in the morning.

Gettysburg's casualties were so overwhelming that the town itself became a vast makeshift hospital. "Every barn, church, and building of any size in Gettysburg had been converted into a temporary hospital," said Cornelia Hancock, a volunteer from New Jersey. "We went . . . to one of the churches, where I saw for the first time what war meant. Hundreds of desperately wounded men were stretched out on boards laid across the high-backed pews as closely as they could be packed together. The boards were covered with straw. Thus elevated, these poor sufferers' faces, white and drawn with pain, were almost on a level with my own. I seemed to stand breast-high in a sea of anguish." Hancock had no nursing experience, so she spent the night writing messages from dying soldiers for their families and friends.

The gory scenes were too much for some volunteer nurses. When Cornelia McDonald offered to help care for wounded Confederates in Winchester, Virginia, a surgeon asked her to wash the face of a wounded Tennessee captain. McDonald took one look at the soldier and nearly fainted. "A ball had struck him on the side of the face, taking away both eyes, and the bridge of his nose," she later recalled. She staggered toward the door, nearly tripping over a pile of amputated arms and legs. "My faintness increased," she said, "and I had to stop and lean against the wall to keep from falling."

In time, most nurses grew accustomed to such scenes. From Gettysburg, Cornelia Hancock wrote to her sister, "I feel assured I shall never feel horrified at anything that may happen to me hereafter. . . . I could stand by and see a man's head taken off I believe—you get so used to it here." Even amputations no longer bothered her. "It is a melancholy sight," she wrote to her mother, "but you have no idea how soon one gets used to it. Their screams of agony do not make as much impression on me as the reading of this letter will on you."

Kate Cumming, a Confederate nurse, felt much the same way after nursing the wounded from the Battle of Shiloh in Tennessee. "The foul air from this mass of human beings at first made me giddy and sick," she wrote in her diary, "but I soon got over it. We have to walk . . . in blood and water; but we think nothing of it at all."

Of the women who were stout-hearted enough to stay, most learned quickly and became skillful nurses. Nevertheless, many male doctors objected to working alongside women, and some behaved like tyrants and tried to make the women miserable. "Hardly a surgeon of whom I can think, received or treated [us] with even common courtesy," said Georgeanna Woolsey, a nurse from New York. One Union surgeon tried to convince a nurse to leave by telling her there was no bed at the hospital for her to sleep in. She stayed anyway, spending her nights in a chair or curled up in a corner. Eventually, some doctors became more tolerant. "They could not do without the women nurses," Woolsey said. "They knew it, and the women knew that they knew it, and so there came to be a tacit understanding about it."

Not every female nurse faced the same hostility. Louisa May Alcott expected to be treated "like a door-mat, a worm, or any other meek and lowly article," but the doctors showed her "the utmost courtesy and kindness," she said. Doctors on both sides often praised the work of Catholic nuns who worked as nurses. More than six hundred nuns volunteered in army hospitals during the war. Some doctors preferred them to other nurses because they were better trained; others favored them because they were more disciplined and obedient.

In general, women who had more responsibility also had more problems with male doctors. Hannah Ropes, the matron of the hospital where Alcott worked, constantly battled with the head surgeon over his sloppy management and the hospital's wretched conditions. He ignored her complaints and treated her like a nuisance. Finally, after getting nowhere with the surgeon's superiors, Ropes took her complaints straight to Edwin Stanton, the U.S. secretary of war. Stanton removed the head surgeon and ordered an official inspection of the hospital.

Like Ropes, many women were frustrated by the cumbersome rules. When they encountered filthy and disorganized hospitals, drunken surgeons, and dishonest officials, they demanded change. Mary Ann Bickerdyke of Illinois, a middle-aged woman who nursed thousands of Union soldiers and was a whirlwind at organizing hospitals, accomplished things by simply charging through barriers. "It's of no use for you to try to tie me up with your red tape," she once told a doctor. "There's too much to be done down here to stop for that."

When Bickerdyke was appointed matron of a large hospital in Cairo, Illinois, she discovered that food and liquor were being stolen by surgeons and wardmasters. She confronted the chief surgeon about the matter, only to have him order her out of the hospital. But she refused to leave. Determined to catch the thieves, she spiked a batch of stewed peaches with medicine that would cause vomiting. Walking in on a group of choking, groaning men, she warned them that the next time she would use rat poison. On another occasion, when Bickerdyke caught a wardmaster wearing a shirt, slippers, and

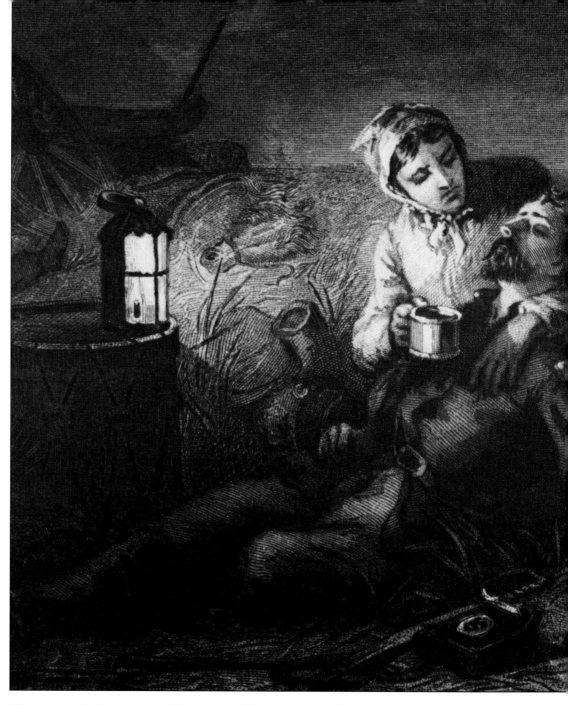

Mary Ann Bickerdyke of Illinois cared for wounded Federal soldiers at nineteen battle sites.

socks meant for the soldiers, she made him strip to his underwear in front of the patients. Mother Bickerdyke, as the soldiers affectionately called her, had little real power, but if anyone challenged her she would answer, "I have received my authority from the Lord God Almighty; have you anything that ranks higher than that?"

Clara Barton, who nursed Union soldiers at several battlefields while running her own one-woman supply operation, refused to work within the official system. Instead, she would load her carriage with food and supplies, and set off to find the wounded troops, often arriving before the fighting had even stopped. Barton was the first nurse on the scene at Antietam, in Maryland, where more than twenty thousand men were killed or wounded. Covered with blood and grime, she moved from soldier to soldier, carving out bullets with her pocketknife and wrapping wounds first with bandages and then with cornhusks when she ran out of cloth. In the evenings, she cooked up enormous kettles of watery stew that the hungry survivors gratefully devoured.

The handful of women doctors found it nearly impossible to fit into the system. Esther Hill Hawks, trained at the New England Female Medical College in Boston, tried to volunteer as an army doctor, but the government refused to hire women for that job. She then applied to be a nurse, but was rejected by Dorothea Dix, probably because she was not yet thirty years old. In late 1862 she was finally accepted as a teacher in Beaufort, South Carolina, where the Union forces had freed thousands of slaves. Her husband, also a doctor, was already working in Beaufort, and in 1863 he became the head of a hospital for black soldiers. He welcomed her help.

The Hawkses' patients included soldiers from the First South Carolina Volunteers, the first official black regiment in the Union Army. In July 1863, one hundred and fifty soldiers from the Fifty-fourth Massachusetts Regiment were brought in after a fierce battle at Fort Wagner, fifty miles to the north. The soldiers were "laid on blankets on the floor all mangled and ghastly," Hawks wrote in her diary. "What a terrible sight it was!" She was surprised to find that the regiment included college graduates as well as former slaves. "They are intelligent, courteous, cheerful and kind, and I pity the humanity which, on a close acquaintance with these men, still retains the unworthy prejudice against color!" she wrote.

All of the women who volunteered for hospital work saw their worlds expand. Many had never ventured beyond their hometowns, and now they suddenly found themselves in strange, but fascinating surroundings. Although they would carry the images of suffering with them for the rest of their lives, they gained a taste of freedom and a sense of pride in serving their country.

Many, like Katharine Wormeley, who worked aboard a Union hospital ship, later remembered the war as the most exciting time of their lives. Wormeley felt she had lived an entire lifetime during her three months of duty. Sitting on deck as the ship waited for another load of wounded, she hurriedly finished off a letter to a friend. "Good-bye!" she wrote. *This is life.* ◆

A nurse from the Armory Square Hospital in Washington, D.C., measures medicine.

Frances Clalin was one of dozens of women who disguised themselves as men and fought in the army. Clalin is shown here in women's dress and in her Union cavalry uniform.

Soldiers and Spies

At first glance, the patient looked like hundreds of other wounded Yankees captured in the Battle of Chickamauga in Tennessee. A shell had torn a gaping wound in the soldier's thigh. But as a Confederate surgeon bent over the patient for a closer look, he realized that something was wrong: This enemy soldier was a woman.

Two days later, the woman was taken across enemy lines and turned over to Union commanders with this message: "As the Confederates do not use women in war, this woman, wounded in battle, is returned to you." She had fought with her company for an entire year, and no one in battle on either side had suspected that she was a woman. She refused to reveal her real name to anyone or tell where she was from, and when a Union nurse asked her why she had enlisted in the army, she replied, "I thought I'd like camp life, and I did."

Dozens of women were discovered posing as male soldiers during the Civil War, and hundreds more may have done so without being discovered. Like the mysterious soldier at Chickamauga, many likely would have gone on fighting if they hadn't been wounded in battle and examined by doctors. Certainly some were killed alongside men in battle and buried with their secret intact.

Women enlisted for many reasons. Some couldn't stand to be separated from the men they loved; others felt they could serve their country best on the battlefield. All were reckless and brave enough to transform themselves into the very opposite of the fragile and feminine ladies they were expected to be. Even with a short haircut, a suit of men's clothes, and a new name, a woman had to be extremely clever to fool her officers and fellow soldiers.

◆ Camp Followers ◆

Women were occasionally allowed to visit army camps once the troops were settled in. Most visitors were officers' wives, who could afford to make the journey. Mary Logan, whose husband was a colonel in the Thirty-first Illinois Regiment, found a whole crowd of other visitors in camp in 1861. "Fathers, mothers, brothers, sisters, wives, and sweethearts came sweeping down in caravans of carriages, wagons, and every conceivable vehicle, and in every

Entire families stayed in army camps. This photograph was taken at the camp of a Pennsylvania regiment.

Franny Wilson of New Jersey fought in the Union Army for eighteen months before she was wounded at Vicksburg, Mississippi, and found out. Amy Clark donned a Confederate uniform to be near her husband, but kept fighting even after he was killed in 1862. Jennie Hodgers fought in an Illinois regiment for four years as Albert Cashier and kept her male disguise for decades after the war. Her real identity was discovered only after she was injured in a car accident in 1911.

When Loreta Velazquez begged her husband, a Confederate

imaginable manner," she said, "pitching their tents and building their brush houses as near the regiment . . . as the commanding officers would permit." When Nancy De Saussure of South Carolina went to camp to visit her husband, a Confederate surgeon, they stayed in a relatively luxurious two-room cabin.

Kady Brownell was the "daughter" of three Rhode Island regiments. Her husband fought in one of them, the First Rhode Island.

Other camp followers included laundresses, prostitutes, and unofficial mascots known as regimental daughters. Regimental daughters lived in camp, marched with the troops, and acted as nurses and friends to the soldiers. Twenty-year-old Eliza Wilson of Wisconsin was typical. She dressed in a handsome uniform and had her own tent and personal servant. She was attached to the Fifth Wisconsin Regiment, which included several of her relatives. Some regimental daughters, such as Kady Brownell of Rhode Island, even found themselves under fire. In 1862, when the First Rhode Island Regiment was traveling through a dense forest, another group of Union soldiers mistook them for the enemy and opened fire. Brownell rushed ahead with the regimental flag and waved it until the attackers realized their mistake.

Loreta Velazquez posing as Harry Buford. Velazquez, who was half Spanish, eloped with a Confederate officer to escape an arranged marriage to a Spaniard.

officer, to bring her with him when he left for war, he refused. Once he left, she disguised herself as a man and even recruited her own battalion. With her thick, dark hair cropped short and a false mustache and beard glued to her face, she decided that she was "an uncommonly good-looking fellow." Calling herself Harry Buford, she pushed her voice as low as she could, put on a manly swagger, and even practiced spitting in the street.

Velazquez's personal accounts of her extraordinary experiences in battle are probably exaggerated, like many reminiscences of the Civil War, but her feelings were genuine. She recalled that serving in battle disguised as a man made her feel like a gambler playing for enormous stakes. The longer she stayed in the army, the more confident she became on the battlefield. "Fear was a word I did not know the meaning of," she said, "and as I noted the ashy faces, and the trembling limbs of some of the men about me, I almost wished I could feel a little fear, if only for the sake of sympathizing with the poor devils."

Velazquez claimed that she was appointed temporary commander of a company during the Battle of Ball's Bluff in Virginia in October 1861, after all the officers had disappeared and were assumed to be dead. When the battle was over and won, however, the first lieutenant appeared, telling Velazquez that he had been taken prisoner by the Yankees but managed to escape. "He had a very sheepish look," she said, "as if he was ashamed of himself for playing a sneaking, cowardly trick. . . ." She was convinced that he had hidden himself away until the fighting was over.

Sarah Edmonds, a Northerner, enjoyed masquerading as a man at least as much as Loreta Velazquez did. A skilled horsewoman who had grown up hunting and fishing with her brothers in Canada, Edmonds never enjoyed the life of a lady. She first disguised herself as a man when she was barely twenty years old, after running away from home to escape an arranged marriage. She moved to Connecticut, took the name Franklin Thompson, and found a job at a publishing company. She later went to Flint, Michigan, where she became known in the community as an upstanding young man with many female admirers.

A month after the war began, Edmonds enlisted in the Second Michigan Volunteer Infantry as a male nurse. She went through basic training with the rest of the recruits, impressing her fellow soldiers with her shooting and riding skills. Her camp buddies thought of her as a tough and energetic young man, and her bunkmate never even suspected that "Frank" was a woman. In the camps, soldiers often slept in their clothes and washed themselves with a quick splash from a basin, so Edmonds was able to hide her true identity.

Loreta Velazquez told numerous stories of her brave deeds. She is shown here leading a charge.

Later in the war, Edmonds became a Union spy. Like Loreta Velazquez, she told wild and likely exaggerated stories of her adventures. She said that on her first spying mission, she darkened her face, neck, and hands and went behind enemy lines posing as a black man. She joined a group of slaves who were building a rebel fort and then took notes on the fort's dimensions and the positions of all the mounted guns.

Sarah Edmonds as Franklin Thompson

On her second day behind rebel lines, Edmonds traded jobs with a slave who fetched water for the soldiers. As she made her way around the rebel camp eavesdropping, she spotted a group of soldiers listening intently to a man speaking in a loud and animated voice. "I went up quietly, put down my cans of water, and of course had to fill the men's canteens," Edmonds later said. "I thought the voice sounded familiar. . . ." Glancing up, she recognized the man as a peddler who came into the Federal camp once a week to sell newspapers and stationery. He was giving a full description of the Union camp, and had a map showing where the Federal forces were positioned. Edmonds could hardly wait to report the spy to her superiors. "He was a fated man from that moment," she later recalled with satisfaction. "His life was not worth three cents. . . ."

Harriet Tubman, the daring woman who led slaves to freedom on the Underground Railroad, was probably better qualified than any white spy to gather information. An ex-slave herself, Tubman recruited a group of former slaves to hunt for rebel camps and report to the Union commanders on Confederate troop movements. Together they roamed the countryside, using the routes she knew so well from her Underground Railroad expeditions.

In 1863 Tubman accompanied Colonel James Montgomery and about one hundred and fifty black soldiers on a gunboat raid along the Combahee River in South Carolina. Tubman and her scouts surveyed the entire area before the raid was launched, asking slaves where Confederate soldiers had placed explosives in the river. With that crucial information, the Union gunboats made their way safely along the zigzagging river, picking off small bands of rebel soldiers along the way. Union troops dashed along both riverbanks not far behind, setting fire to plantations and stores of cotton. The rebels were caught unprepared, and when they realized they were outnumbered, they retreated.

The plantation owners fled, and at first some slaves hid in the nearby woods. But when they learned that the gunboats would take them behind Union lines, they came running to the river from all directions, waving and shouting, and carrying as many belongings as they could. "I never saw such a sight," Tubman later said. One woman came on board with a steaming pot of rice on

After the war, Sarah Edmonds married, gave birth to three children, and adopted two more. Many of her fellow soldiers did not learn of her true identity until twenty years later, when she asked them for help in getting a military pension.

her head, a pig slung across her back, and three or four children clinging to her dress. Another brought along a black pig she called Jeff Davis, named for the Confederate president.

The strategy of spying in familiar country worked equally well for Rose O'Neal Greenhow, a wealthy, southern-born widow who lived in Washington, D.C. Tall and dark-haired with piercing black eyes and a theatrical style, Greenhow was an influential society hostess in the capital. Her elegant home on Sixteenth Street drew a continual stream of rich and powerful visitors—senators, government officials, and military leaders. Many of her friends left

---

♦ **Crazy Betsy** ♦

Elizabeth Van Lew spied for the Union Army from a magnificent mansion on Grace Street in Richmond, the Confederate capital. The daughter of a successful hardware merchant, Van Lew was educated in Philadelphia, where she acquired strong antislavery views. When her father died, she and her mother freed all the family slaves. So uncommon was her behavior that her neighbors called her Crazy Betsy.

Van Lew reported to Union generals on conditions in the Confederate capital, and turned her home into a hideout for escapees from Confederate prisons. She had a secret room in her house, reachable only by a hidden staircase. She once kept one hundred men there after they dug their way out of Richmond's Libby Prison. She also visited prisons, with the excuse of donating food, and collected valuable information from the inmates.

Van Lew relied on help from hired black servants to carry coded messages out of town, and she sometimes hid notes inside an empty eggshell in a basket of produce. In one of her bolder moves, she managed to install one of her former slaves as a servant in the home of Jefferson Davis to spy on the Confederate president. After the war, General Ulysses S. Grant rewarded Van Lew for her services by appointing her postmistress of Richmond. Although she was shunned by all her neighbors, she remained in Richmond until she died in 1900.

Washington in 1861 to join the Confederacy, but Greenhow stayed behind, using her social connections to spy for the South.

In early July 1861, Greenhow learned that the Union's General Irvin McDowell was planning to attack southern troops near Manassas, Virginia. Once she found out how many troops were with McDowell, and even which roads they planned to take, she sent a young friend into Virginia on a vegetable wagon, disguised as a farm girl. Her coded message for the Confederate General Pierre Gustave Toutant Beauregard was hidden in the young woman's hair, rolled into a tiny coil. Eleven days later, with the help of Greenhow's advance warning, Beauregard won a major victory at Manassas.

Eventually, rumors of Greenhow's spying activities reached Federal agents. They watched her house, and on a muggy night in August, they saw a Union officer enter and pull out what looked like a military map. The two were arrested, and the agents ransacked Greenhow's home, looking for evidence. "My beds, drawers, and wardrobes were all upturned," she said, "soiled clothes were . . . mercilessly exposed; papers that had not seen the light for years were dragged forth." No military secrets were found, but the agents did discover a bundle of love letters from a northern senator.

Greenhow's home was placed under twenty-four-hour guard, but with help from friends who came to visit, she continued collecting and passing information to the South. Finally, she was moved to the Old Capitol Prison, where she was kept for more than a year.

When Greenhow was released and sent to the South, she was welcomed as a heroine. She traveled to Europe soon after to raise money and drum up support for the Confederacy. On the way home, her ship ran aground off the coast of North Carolina in a heavy storm. She tried to get ashore in a rowboat, but it capsized. Weighted down with gold sewn into her clothing, Greenhow drowned.

Not long after after Rose Greenhow had left the Old Capitol Prison, a young woman named Belle Boyd was imprisoned there for spying. Charming and headstrong, Boyd seemed to be as talented at getting into trouble as she was at spying. When she was only seventeen, she shot a drunken Yankee soldier who had insulted her mother.

Rose O'Neal Greenhow was visited by her daughter in the Old Capitol Prison.

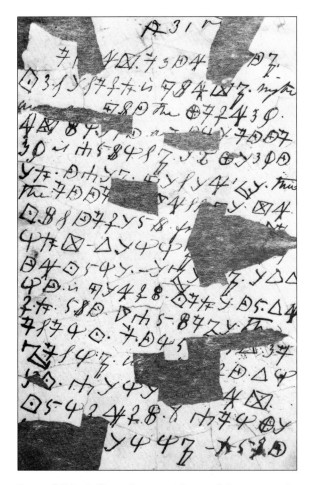

**Rose O'Neal Greenhow used an elaborate code
to send messages to Confederate commanders.**

Boyd used all of her cunning to befriend and spy on Union soldiers when they occupied her hometown of Martinsburg, Virginia, early in the war. But she was not nearly as sophisticated as Rose Greenhow. Boyd wrote her messages in longhand, and signed her name at the bottom. Before long, one of them was intercepted and she was arrested. At the prison, Boyd caused a stir, as always. She tried to annoy her captors by singing "Take Me Back to the Sunny South" and hanging a portrait of Jefferson Davis in her cell. She was released after a month and immediately went back to work as a spy and courier. She was arrested again and served a second prison term in Washington. Toward the end of

Belle Boyd, the glamorous Confererate spy who was twice jailed in Washington, D.C.

the war, she fell in love with a Yankee officer and converted him to the Confederate cause. They were married, but he died soon after, leaving Boyd a widow at the age of twenty-one. After the war, she embarked on a second career, giving dramatic accounts of her wartime exploits while dressed in a splendid uniform of Confederate gray. ♦

Letters were the primary form of communication between women and their loved ones in the army. As the war dragged on, much of the news that reached the home front was tragic.

This Cruel War

Soon after the Battle of Five Forks in Virginia, word reached LaSalle Pickett in Richmond that her husband, General George Pickett, had been killed. At home with her baby, she paced the floor, wondering if the rumors were true, when a newsboy called out from the street, "Grand victory at Five Forks! Pickett killed and his whole division captured!"

Several sleepless nights followed, as LaSalle Pickett waited for official word of her husband's death. Then, one morning, as she stood by an upstairs window, she heard a horse trot up to the house and a familiar voice say, "Whoa, Lucy." It was her husband. "How I got down the stairs I do not know," she later said. "I do not know how to describe the peace, the bliss of that moment—it is too deep and too sacred to be translated into words."

It was hard for women not to believe rumors. News of the war reached the home front in fragments and often took weeks or even months to arrive. Those left at home pieced together what they could from letters, newspapers, and hearsay. In Massachusetts, Harriet Beecher Stowe found out from the morning paper that her son Fred had been wounded in the head at the Battle of

Gettysburg. Kate Stone, a twenty-two-year-old woman from Louisiana, didn't learn of her brother's death from disease until nearly two months after it happened.

By the second year of the war, when tens of thousands of men were dying sometimes in a single day, there was hardly an American family left that wasn't mourning the death of a relative or friend. In November 1862, an Iowa woman learned from a single letter that her husband, father, and brother had all been killed in battle.

Mary Chesnut of South Carolina described what it was like to receive the dreaded news. "A telegram comes to you," she said, "and you leave it in your lap. You are pale with fright. You handle it, or dread to touch it, as you would a rattlesnake—worse—worse. A snake would only strike you." Chesnut knew a woman who lost her child to illness and then learned that her husband had died. "She did not utter one word," Chesnut said. "She remained quiet so long, someone removed the light shawl which she had drawn over her head. She was dead."

Mary Chesnut's diary became a long list of deaths, and not just of soldiers. "Grief and constant anxiety kill nearly as many women as men die on the battlefield," she said. Women died in childbirth, and epidemics of smallpox and scarlet fever claimed many civilians. Medicine became scarce as the army used up most of the supplies.

Shortages were worse in the South due to the Union's blockade of southern ports. While some goods were smuggled in, not even the wealthiest Southerners could afford to eat or dress as they liked. Kate Stone, a stylish belle before the war, said in 1862, "Fashion is an obsolete word and just to be decently clad is all we expect." White women made dresses out of the rough fabric ordinarily worn by slaves, and fashioned shoes out of old carpets, canvas sails, belts, and even saddles. One Alabama society woman noted that needles had become "precious as heirlooms" and pins were "the rarest of luxuries."

Women on farms and plantations experimented with dogwood berries, blackberry roots, and other herbs to treat illness. Corncobs were burned to ash and used in place of soda to make bread rise. Just about everyone gave up coffee, as the scarce beans cost

◆ **My Dear Girl** ◆

Women waited anxiously for word from their men in the army, knowing that each letter could be the last. Amelia Loguen of Syracuse, New York, received this letter in 1863 from her sweetheart, Lewis Douglass, a volunteer in the all-black Fifty-fourth Massachusetts Regiment and the son of the famous abolitionist Frederick Douglass. He wrote to her from South Carolina after a battle in which his regiment lost one-third of its men.

Morris Island S.C.   July 20

My Dear Amelia:

I have been in two fights, and am unhurt. I am about to go in another I believe to-night. Our men fought well on both occasions. The last was desperate we charged that terrible battery on Morris Island known as Fort Wagner. . . . I escaped unhurt from amidst that perfect hail of shot and shell. It was terrible. . . .

My thoughts are with you often, you are as dear as ever, be good enough to remember it as I no doubt you will. As I said before we are on the eve of another fight and I am very busy and have just snatched a moment to write to you. I must necessarily be brief. Should I fall in the next fight killed or wounded I hope I fall with my face to the foe. . . .

This regiment has established its reputation as a fighting regiment not a man flinched, though it was a trying time. Men fell all around me. A shell would explode and clear a space of twenty feet, our men would close up again, but it was no use we had to retreat, which was a very hazardous undertaking. How I got out of that fight alive I cannot tell, but I am here. My Dear girl I hope again to see you. I must bid you farewell should I be killed. Remember if I die I die in a good cause. I wish we had a hundred thousand colored troops we would put an end to this war. Good Bye to all.

Your own loving   *Write soon*

Lewis

Lewis Douglass survived the war and married Amelia Loguen.

Southern women made daring smuggling expeditions to bring medicine, weapons, and other scarce items into the blockaded South. Here, Yankee soldiers find a stash of boots hidden under a woman's hoop skirt.

as much as seventy dollars a pound. In its place, they made dark brews from browned okra seeds, toasted yams, and burnt corn. In Petersburg, Virginia, bacon and butter cost twenty dollars a pound by early 1865. Chickens were fifty dollars each. In Columbia, South Carolina, Mary Chesnut paid fifty dollars for a small wooden bucket that would have cost no more than twenty-five cents before the war.

The war also brought hardship in the North. Most married soldiers sent home part of their wages—they earned about thirteen dollars a month—but the army was often late in paying the troops. Women took jobs in factories and shops just to earn enough to provide food for their children. But they earned less than men did in the same jobs, and to keep up with rising prices, some had to put their children to work as well. In Philadelphia, by the end of the war one out of every five textile workers was under age sixteen.

In both the North and South, workers of all types were in short supply. Some women took up tedious and often dangerous work in weapons factories, making shells and cartridges; others became clerks in government offices. Farming communities were among the hardest hit by labor shortages. In some places, more than half the men of military age had joined the army, leaving women to work the fields in addition to doing their usual tasks of cooking, cleaning, tending the livestock, and raising their children. When Mary Livermore of the Chicago Sanitary Commission traveled through the Iowa countryside to organize soldiers' aid societies, she found women driving the reapers and loading grain. Those same women somehow also found time to sew clothes and roll bandages for the troops.

For the women and children left behind, home life felt empty and lonely. Rachel Cormany of Pennsylvania kept busy caring for her young daughter, but at times the strain of being apart from her husband Samuel, a Union soldier, overwhelmed her. "Tears relieve me very much," she wrote in her diary. "My heart always seems lighter after weeping freely." On their wedding anniversary in 1863, after Samuel had been gone for more than a year, she felt completely despondent. "Our third Marriage Anniversary. A bright clear cold day," she wrote. "Just one like the

♦   Bread or Blood   ♦

Wartime shortages drove prices so high in the South that many people could not afford to buy food or other necessities even when they were available. The situation was made worse by greedy merchants who hoarded food in order to charge higher prices.

In overcrowded Richmond, hungry citizens became desperate. On April 2, 1863, a woman named Mary Jackson led a group of three hundred armed women into the stores, demanding food at the same prices that the army paid. When their demands were ignored, they simply took what they wanted, declaring that they would have "bread or blood."

The women were soon joined by excited bystanders, and the crowd turned into a violent mob. Windows were smashed, and doors were broken down. Shoe stores, bakeries, and groceries were completely emptied in a matter of minutes. The governor arrived on the scene, but failed to control the mob. Finally, President Jefferson Davis was called out. Standing on a cart to address the crowd, he pulled out his watch and declared that he would order troops to open fire if the people did not leave in five minutes. The crowd dispersed. Mary Jackson and about fifty others were later arrested.

After the riot, prices were lowered for a time in Richmond, but the problem of shortages only grew worse as the war went on. Other cities faced the same difficulties, and "bread riots" took place in Atlanta, Raleigh, Petersburg, Mobile, Savannah, New Orleans, and several other cities.

This unflattering depiction of a southern bread riot appeared in a northern newspaper. In the South, many newspapers refused to report on the riots, for fear of demoralizing Southerners.

wedding day was. Then I was happy. . . . A bright future was looming up before me. . . . Now clouds arose to overshadow our bright skies. . . ."

In spite of all the hardships, social life continued during the war, especially among the upper classes. In Richmond and Co-

Women joined the work force in increasing numbers during the war, especially in the war industries. Massachusetts women are shown here making cartridges for the Union Army.

lumbia, Mary Chesnut never gave up her busy schedule of dinners and tea parties. Top Confederate Army officers, including Mary's husband, James Chesnut, Jr., swept in and out of town between battles. General John Bell Hood visited the Chesnuts often enough to court Mary's beautiful friend Buck Preston. Hood

returned to Richmond in 1863 with only one leg. Chesnut noted a startling array of injuries at a gathering that Christmas in Columbia. Army men "dropped in after dinner, without arms, without legs," she said. One guest couldn't speak because of a wound in his throat. Another had lost an eye.

One of the foremost concerns of Mary Chesnut and her fellow slaveowners was the behavior of their slaves. Chesnut watched her servants closely and wondered if they realized that their freedom was at stake in the war. Some slaveowners grew terrified that their slaves would try to poison them, and rumors of slave revolts created an atmosphere of panic. Some Southerners were so nervous about their slaves running off to join the Yankees that they put them in shackles.

About half a million slaves did find refuge behind Union lines. Some made their way to Federal camps near their homes; others escaped farther north to free states. These former slaves became known as contrabands, because the Union Army declared them to be seized property, like buildings, weapons, and forts taken from the enemy in battle. Washington, D.C., became especially crowded with contrabands during the war. They arrived with great hopes, but their first taste of freedom was soon made bitter by hunger, cold, illness, and the realization that they were not welcome. "Many good friends reached forth kind hands, but the North is not warm and impulsive," said Elizabeth Keckley, a former slave who was a dressmaker for prominent women in Washington. "For one kind word spoken, two harsh ones were uttered."

But despite the hardships they faced, many contrabands served the Union cause in important ways. Tens of thousands of contraband men fought for the Union Army, and contraband women served as army nurses, camp cooks, and laundresses. Susie King, a former slave from Georgia, worked as a laundress for four years and three months without pay in a Union regiment made up of contraband men. King, who joined up to be near her husband, uncles, and cousins, also taught the soldiers to read and write and nursed the wounded after battle.

Blacks were not the only refugees of the war. More than a quarter million white Southerners fled their homes to escape the invading Yankees. Most were women and children. Some ran off

Slaves who sought protection from Union forces often traveled from camp to camp with the soldiers. This group of escaped slaves fords the Rappahannock River in Virginia in August 1862 to stay with the Federal forces.

◆ To See This Day ◆

Outside of Washington, D.C., the largest group of contrabands was on South Carolina's Sea Islands. When the Union Army captured the islands in late 1861, the plantation owners fled, leaving behind ten thousand slaves. When word spread that the islands had been liberated, slaves from all over the South made their way there.

The Sea Island slaves lived in very harsh conditions, and the other slaves who fled to the islands arrived hungry, sick, and exhausted. When news of the contrabands' condition reached the North, concerned citizens formed "freedmen's aid societies" to send money, clothing, and medicine. With the government's help, they also sent volunteer teachers. If the Sea Island contrabands could be educated and could survive in freedom, these Northerners argued, then the whole world would see how wrong the South was for treating them as property.

Teachers began arriving in the spring of 1862. A quarter of them were women. Many, like twenty-four-year-old Charlotte Forten, a free black woman, were passionate abolitionists. For them, the Sea Island experiment represented the glorious beginning of a new era. The day after Forten arrived on Ladies Island, she awoke to the sound of voices in the yard outside. "We ran to the window, and looked out," she wrote in her diary. "Women in bright colored handkerchiefs, some carrying pails on their heads, were crossing the yard, busy with their morning work; children were playing and tumbling around them. On every face there was a look of serenity and cheerfulness. . . . I thanked God that I had lived to see this day."

Charlotte Forten came from a family of leading Philadelphia abolitionists. Some of her relatives were stationkeepers on the Underground Railroad. Forten devoted her life to teaching and to working for civil rights.

One of the highlights of Forten's eight-month stay was a visit with Harriet Tubman, who turned up on the islands to help feed and nurse the contrabands. Some were slaves she had helped liberate during the Union gunboat raid on the nearby Combahee River. "She is a wonderful woman—a real heroine," Forten wrote. Tubman told her the story of a slave named Joe, who she led to freedom. He was silent and moody the entire trip, and when they crossed a suspension bridge into Canada over a brilliant waterfall, he wouldn't even look at it. But when Tubman told him, "Now we are in

A school for contraband children in Beaufort, on Port Royal Island

Canada," he sprang up and danced wildly, shouting and clapping his hands. "My own eyes were full as I listened to her," Forten wrote. "And to hear her sing the very scraps of jubilant hymns that he sang. . . . I am glad I saw her— *very* glad."

Forten and the other Northerners faced a bewildering task. Many of their students were frail and sickly, and wore rags for clothes. Most had never been to school, and some didn't even know what a book was, or how to hold one. One teacher, Elizabeth Botume, discovered that the contraband children were afraid of her because she was white. When she first arrived at the rough wooden schoolhouse where she was assigned to teach, the porch was filled with children playing and laughing. "But as soon as they saw me they all gave a whoop and a bound and disappeared," she said.

Another teacher, Mary Ames, started out with fifteen students and saw her class grow to more than a hundred in less than a month. She taught the children the alphabet and numbers, and several songs—their favorite was "Hang Jeff Davis to a Sour Apple Tree." In the evenings, adults came to her for lessons after a full day of work in the fields.

The northern teachers were proud of the progress that their students made under such trying conditions. Many wrote articles and books to spread the word that the Sea Island experiment was succeeding. Because of their accomplishments, thousands of other Northerners—including four thousand women—went south after the war to teach the freed people. "My experiences are but one leaf in the history of emancipation," wrote Elizabeth Botume, who taught on the islands for several years. "There is nothing in the history of the world which . . . can compare with the progress of events since 'freedom was declared.'"

to live with relatives in the countryside, others set out for cities less likely to be attacked. Taking all the valuables they could carry—jewelry, furs, china, even furniture—they left their homes on foot, on mules, and in wagons. Sometimes thousands of frenzied Southerners would clog a single dirt road leading out of town.

Many tried to leave by train. One woman who caught a train at Macon, Georgia, described the scene at the station as "a ter-

Contrabands were often put to work by Union officers, doing washing, cooking, and even hard labor. Here, a group of contrabands washes clothing for the troops.

rible rush on all the outgoing trains. People who could not get inside were hanging on wherever they could find a sticking place," she said. "The aisles and platforms down to the last step were full of people clinging on like bees swarming round the doors of a hive."

As they fled, the refugees slept wherever they could find shelter—in carriage houses, stables, slave cabins, or empty railroad cars. They crowded into the major southern cities of Atlanta, Richmond, and Columbia, making housing and supply shortages even worse.

In May 1862, Sarah Morgan fled Baton Rouge under a shower of Yankee shells. When the bombardment began, she was still rushing around her house, deciding what to take with her. She

Georgia refugees flee from the advancing Union Army.

Many refugees took their most valued possessions with them. They were often forced to sell their belongings to buy food or abandon them when road conditions became too rugged.

and her mother were afraid they would not get out of the house alive. "As we stood in the door, four or five shells sailed over our heads at the same time, seeming to make a perfect corkscrew of the air," Morgan said. Hitching a ride on a friend's wagon, they joined the stream of terrified people pouring out of the city. "It was a heart-rending scene," she said. "Women searching for their babies along the road, where they had been lost; others sitting in the dust crying and wringing their hands."

Three months later, an even fiercer battle took place in the heart of Baton Rouge. Awakened by firing in the streets and windows being shattered by gunfire, more people fled their homes. From a plantation house on the Mississippi River overlooking the city, Eliza McHatton watched as a crowd of people stumbled toward her plantation. They were a pathetic sight, she said—"hatless, bonnetless, some with slippers and no stockings, some with wrappers hastily thrown over nightgowns. Now and then a coatless man on a bare-back horse holding a helpless child in his arms, and a terrified woman clinging on behind."

They poured through the plantation gates and under trellises braided with honeysuckle and jasmine. The broad lawn, dotted with live-oak and pecan trees, was soon covered with "about five hundred tired, exhausted, broken-down, sick, frightened, terrified human beings," McHatton said. She went to work making tea and in a few hours had used up twelve pounds of tea leaves, which she steeped in immense iron kettles ordinarily used for making soap.

The Confederate Army lost that battle in Baton Rouge, and several days later McHatton went into town to see what was left of it. Walking into one of the finest homes in the city, she found portraits on the walls slashed from side to side, cupboards split open, and splintered china scattered across the floor. Molasses and vinegar were smeared over the walls and furniture.

By the end of the year, McHatton and her husband had packed up their belongings and left for safer territory in Texas. They had seen enough destruction. They could hardly have imagined that the war would rage three more years and that what had happened to Baton Rouge was just the beginning of the devastation of the cities and farmlands of the South. ♦

Residents of Columbia, South Carolina, blamed drunken Union soldiers
for setting the city ablaze. However, some of the fires may have been
started by Confederates trying to burn bales of cotton before the enemy
arrived.

SIX

The Road to Peace

On the night of February 17, 1865, seventeen-year-old Emma LeConte watched from her back porch as the city of Columbia, South Carolina, was destroyed by fire. "Imagine night turning into noonday," she wrote in her diary, "only with a blazing, scorching glare that was horrible—a copper colored sky across which swept columns of black rolling smoke glittering with sparks and flying embers. . . ."

Columbia was one stop along the path of destruction known as Sherman's March. Union General William Tecumseh Sherman's troops had burned and looted their way through Georgia and were heading through South Carolina, the birthplace of the Confederate rebellion. Sherman's soldiers were determined to break the spirit of the southern people, and to destroy everything along their way that could be useful to the Confederate Army. "It was like the path stripped by a tornado, narrow but complete destruction in it," one South Carolina woman said.

The night that Sherman's troops entered Columbia, the city was full of refugees, mostly women and children, as well as its own population. Emma LeConte watched as the flames jumped from building to building, whipped along by a fierce winter wind.

"Every instant came the crashing of timbers and the thunder of falling buildings," she said. "A quivering molten ocean seemed to fill the air and sky."

In the countryside, Sherman's troops took what they wanted from farms and storehouses. They had been ordered not to attack civilians or destroy their property, but some soldiers went ahead and set fire to homes and even attacked and raped women.

On one South Carolina rice plantation, Elizabeth Pringle and

About half of the buildings in Columbia were destroyed in a single night.

her mother buried their valuables in the woods and poured all of their whiskey into a stream when they heard that the Yankees were approaching. They also ate all the food they could so the enemy wouldn't get it. "Every day we had a real Christmas dinner," Pringle said. "All the turkeys and hams were used."

One evening, as they sat down for dinner, the Yankees arrived. A group of soldiers burst into the house, shouting, "We want whiskey! We want firearms!" Crowding around the table,

the soldiers devoured a roast turkey and all the trimmings, then headed for the storeroom. Pringle's mother let them in with a key so they wouldn't break the door down. The men pawed through box after box, finding no liquor. Then, in the very last box one of the soldiers discovered a bottle and shouted, "You were lying!" Putting the bottle to his lips, he took a big swallow. "Then there was a splutter and choking," Pringle recalled, "and he got rid of it as quickly as he could. It was our one treasured bottle of olive-oil, which had been put out of reach, to be kept for some great occasion."

On April 3, 1865, after Sherman's troops had left a three-hundred-mile trail of rubble through the heart of the Confederacy, Union soldiers moved into the southern capital of Richmond, Virginia. After nearly four years of fierce fighting, the Confederacy was on the verge of collapse. "Exactly at eight o'clock the Confederate flag that fluttered above the Capitol came down and the Stars and Stripes were run up," one Richmond woman wrote in her diary. "We knew what that meant! . . . We covered our faces and cried aloud. All through the house was the sound of sobbing."

In the North, with the end of the war clearly in sight, the celebrations began. "Monday came the news of the taking of Richmond. Every body was wild," Sarah Hale of Boston wrote to her son. "Boston was a perfect jubilee—all business was at a stand and music and flags and fireworks in the evening were every where."

The war that most people thought would last just a few months was finally coming to a close. Six days later, General Robert E. Lee, commander of the Confederate Army, surrendered to the Union forces at Appomattox Court House in Virginia. The North and South were once again a single, but torn and devastated nation. The cost was high. Some six hundred thousand were killed on the battlefield, or died in hospitals, prisons, and camps.

Many white southern women were relieved to see the war end, but the loss made them bitter. Nancy De Saussure, a South Carolina refugee, was taking a stroll on a friend's estate when she heard someone call out, "The war is over, Lee has surrendered." She was filled with a confusing mix of emotions. "Joy and sorrow strove with each other," she later recalled. "Joy in the hope of having my husband . . . return to me, but oh, such sorrow over our defeat!" She was a wealthy slaveowner before the war. Now she was penniless, and when she returned to her plantation, she found her home in ruins and her slaves gone. To earn money, she baked apple pies and bread to sell to the Yankees.

Emma LeConte of Columbia was despondent when her cousins, Johnny and Julian, returned from the army. "We would have waited many years if only we could have received them back triumphant," she wrote. "For four years we have looked forward to this day—the day when the troops would march home. We expected to meet them exulting and victorious." Instead, the troops

The people of Washington, D.C., celebrated the end of the war with a victory parade along Pennsylvania Avenue.

came home ragged, maimed, and forlorn, looking nothing like the dashing soldiers who had marched off to war four years earlier.

Katie Rowe, a young slave on a cotton plantation, didn't learn that the war was over until a white man in a broad, black hat came riding up to the plantation and gathered the slaves around him nearly two months after Lee's surrender. Katie assumed that she and the other slaves had all been sold, but then she noticed some of the older slaves smiling. "This is the fourth day of June, and this is 1865," the man said, "and I want you all to remember the date. . . . Today you are free, just like I am, and Mr. Saunders and your mistress and all us white people."

"No one knew where to go," Rowe remembered, "so they all stayed." Her former master divided his land into plots for the freed slaves to farm, but when the cotton was harvested, he took away most of it as payment for their housing and food. Without money or property of their own, many freed slaves had no way to survive other than to work for their former owners. Some were forced to sign labor contracts that kept them virtually enslaved.

Four million slaves were liberated at the end of the war, and many went in search of family members who had been sold away from them years before. "I knew of dozens of children who started out to search through the southland for their parents who had been sold 'down the river,'" said Jennie Hill, a freed Missouri slave. She knew of only one family that had been reunited. A former slave named Sarah Fitzpatrick recalled a similar scene in Alabama. "Husbands looking for their wives, and wives looking for their husbands, children looking for parents, parents looking for children—everything sure was scrambled up in those days," she said.

Families of soldiers faced a similar ordeal when their men did not return home. In the final months of the war, Clara Barton realized that more than half of the Union dead had been buried in unmarked graves, and thousands had died in prison camps. She asked President Lincoln to authorize her to conduct an official search, and he agreed, issuing an announcement that families of missing Union soldiers should write to Barton.

With Lincoln's blessing, and her own money, Barton began her search, working from a small army tent in Annapolis, Maryland. Within two months, she had received thousands of letters,

LECTURE!

MISS CLARA BARTON,

OF WASHINGTON,

THE HEROINE OF ANDERSONVILLE,

The Soldier's Friend, who gave her time and fortune during the war to the Union cause, and who is now engaged in searching for the missing soldiers of the Union army, will address the people of

LAMBERTVILLE, in

HOLCOMBE HALL,

THIS EVENING,

APRIL 7TH, AT 7½ O'CLOCK.

SUBJECT:

SCENES ON THE BATTLE-FIELD.

ADMISSION, 25 CENTS.

Clara Barton lectured widely on her wartime experiences while carrying on her search for missing Union soldiers.

and more were arriving at the rate of a hundred per day. For scores of heartbroken families, Barton was the only hope they had of learning what had happened to their men. "People tell me the color of hair & eyes of the friends they have lost, as if I were expected to go about the country and search them," Barton said.

The names of missing men were organized by state, then published in newspapers and posted in public places. With every list was an appeal to army veterans to write to Barton with any information they had. Thousands wrote to her, describing how friends had fallen on the battlefield or wasted away in prison. By the time she ended her search four years later, she had learned the fate of more than twenty-two thousand Union soldiers.

The war left many families with bitterness and sorrow, just as it left the North and South with a legacy of hatred and destruction to overcome before Americans could again think of themselves as a united country. In Boston, the abolitionist Angelina Grimké sent money and clothing to her sisters in Charleston when she learned that they were surviving on hominy and water. She had worried about her family during the war. Now in her sixties and in failing health, Grimké continued to help the newly freed slaves by speaking at meetings and collecting money.

One evening in 1868, she read an article on "Negroes and the Higher Studies" in a northern newspaper. It mentioned an outstanding young student named Archibald Grimké at Lincoln University, a black college in Pennsylvania. He was a former slave who had earned a reputation as an eloquent speaker. Curious and troubled, Angelina wrote him a letter. "My maiden name was Grimké," she told him, "& as this name is a very uncommon one it occurred to me that you had been probably the slave of one of my brothers & I feel a great desire to know all about you."

In less than a week, she received a reply. "Dear Madam," the letter began. "I am the son of Henry Grimké." The young man was her nephew—the son of her brother Henry, who had died fifteen years earlier. In addition to his white children, Archibald wrote, Henry Grimké had three sons by a slave woman. Archibald was the eldest. When Henry died, he left them to his white son Montague, and they became his house slaves. Archibald escaped from Montague in 1862 and spent the rest of the war in hiding with a free black family.

Angelina was devastated by the story. Although she remembered Henry's cruelty as a young man, she had always loved her brother and hoped that he would change. For the next few months she sent a flurry of letters to Archibald and his brother Francis, asking them for every detail of their lives.

Angelina and her husband embraced her nephews as members of the family, and took an eager interest in their education. When Archibald and Francis graduated from Lincoln University with top

Archibald and Francis Grimké were slaves in the home of their half-brother, Montague Grimké.

honors, Angelina attended to represent the family. "Is it not remarkable that these young men should far exceed in talents any of my other Grimké nephews. . . ." she told a friend. In addition to her teaching job at a girls' school, she worked other jobs to help pay for Archibald's tuition at Harvard Law School and for Francis' at Princeton Theological Seminary.

Forty years after her hatred of slavery forced her to leave the

◆ Women's Rights ◆

The women's rights movement was interrupted during the war, when most of its leaders turned their attention to war-related work. But the Civil War brought about important changes in women's lives, which ultimately strengthened the movement. Thousands of women worked outside their homes during the war, many became heads of households, and most participated in some kind of aid work. In the process, they gained a sense of independence and expanded the sphere of activity that was considered acceptable for women.

After the war, the main goal of the women's rights crusade was to win the right to vote. In 1869, the Fifteenth Amendment was passed, granting black men the right to vote but excluding women. When Sojourner Truth, a leading abolitionist and women's rights activist, realized what was about to happen, she was enraged. "There is a great stir about colored men getting their rights," she said, "but not a word about the colored women; and if colored men get their rights, and not colored women theirs, you see the colored men will be masters over the women, and it will be just as bad as it was before." Women did not gain the right to vote until 1920, more than fifty years later.

Women's rights activists were widely criticized for trying to expand opportunities for women. This 1869 cartoon makes fun of the women's movement by showing men and women in reversed roles.

In 1878, Francis Grimké married Charlotte Forten (seated, holding a book), the abolitionist and teacher of freed slaves on the South Carolina Sea Islands. Their wedding was attended by many leaders of the antislavery movement.

South, Angelina Grimké finally felt at peace with her family. With her help and inspiration, her nephews carried on her work for the rights of blacks and women. "I am glad you have taken the name of Grimké," she told them. "It was once one of the noblest names of Carolina. You, my young friends, now bear this *once* honored name. I charge you most solemnly . . . to lift this name out of the dust where it now lies, and set it once more among the princes of our land." ◆

Bibliography

Alcott, Louisa May. *Hospital Sketches*. New York: Sagamore Press, 1957.

Ames, Mary. *From a New England Woman's Diary in Dixie in 1865*. New York: Negro Universities Press, 1969.

Anderson, John Q., ed. *Brokenburn: The Journal of Kate Stone, 1861–1868*. Baton Rouge: Louisiana State University Press, 1972.

Billington, Ray Allen, ed. *The Journal of Charlotte Forten*. New York: Collier Books, 1961.

Botume, Elizabeth Hyde. *First Days Amongst the Contrabands*. New York: Arno Press and The New York Times, 1968.

Brumgardt, John R., ed. *Civil War Nurse: The Diary and Letters of Hannah Ropes*. Knoxville: University of Tennessee Press, 1980.

Ceplair, Larry, ed. *The Public Years of Sarah and Angelina Grimké: Selected Writings 1835–1839*. New York: Columbia University Press, 1989.

Clinton, Catherine. *The Other Civil War: American Women in the 19th Century*. New York: Hill and Wang, 1984.

————. *The Plantation Mistress: Woman's World in the Old South*. New York: Pantheon Books, 1982.

Conrad, Earl. *Harriet Tubman, Negro Soldier and Abolitionist*. New York: Paul S. Eriksson, 1943.

Dannett, Sylvia G. L., ed. *Noble Women of the North*. New York: Thomas Yoseloff, 1959.

Fauset, Arthur Huff. *Sojourner Truth*. New York: Russell & Russell, 1971.

Fox-Genovese, Elizabeth. *Within the Plantation Household: Black and White Women of the Old South*. Chapel Hill: University of North Carolina Press, 1988.

Hersh, Blanche Glassman. *The Slavery of Sex: Feminist-Abolitionists in America*. Urbana: University of Illinois Press, 1978.

Jones, Katharine M. *Heroines of Dixie: Confederate Women Tell Their Story of the War*. Indianapolis: The Bobbs-Merrill Company, 1955.

Keckley, Elizabeth. *Behind the Scenes. Or, Thirty Years a Slave, and Four Years in the White House*. New York: Oxford University Press, 1988.

Lerner, Gerda. *The Grimké Sisters From South Carolina: Pioneers For Women's Rights and Abolition*. Boston: Houghton Mifflin Co., 1967.

Massey, Mary Elizabeth. *Bonnet Brigades*. New York: Alfred A. Knopf, 1966.

——————. *Refugee Life in the Confederacy*. Baton Rouge: Louisiana State University Press, 1964.

Miers, Earl Schenck, ed. *When the World Ended: The Diary of Emma LeConte*. New York: Oxford University Press, 1957.

Muhlenfeld, Elisabeth. *Mary Boykin Chesnut: A Biography*. Baton Rouge: Louisiana State University Press, 1981.

Myerson, Joel, and Daniel Shealy, eds. *The Journals of Louisa May Alcott*. Boston: Little, Brown and Company, 1989.

Pryor, Elizabeth Brown. *Clara Barton, Professional Angel*. Philadelphia: University of Pennsylvania Press, 1987.

Schwartz, Gerald, ed. *A Woman Doctor's Civil War: Esther Hill Hawks' Diary*. Columbia: University of South Carolina Press, 1984.

Taylor, Susie King. *Reminiscences of My Life in Camp*. New York: Arno Press, 1968.

White, Deborah Gray. *Ar'n't I a Woman?: Female Slaves in the Plantation South*. New York: W. W. Norton & Co., 1985.

Wiley, Bell Irvin. *Confederate Women*. Westport, Conn.: Greenwood Press, 1975.

Woodward, C. Vann, ed. *Mary Chesnut's Civil War*. New Haven, Conn.: Yale University Press, 1981.

——————, and Elisabeth Muhlenfeld, eds. *The Private Mary Chesnut: The Unpublished Civil War Diaries*. New York: Oxford University Press, 1984.

Young, Agatha. *The Women and the Crisis: Women of the North in the Civil War*. New York: McDowell, Oblensky, 1959.

Acknowledgments

I am grateful to numerous research institutions for access to source materials and photographic images that were essential to this book. I would particularly like to thank the librarians and archivists at the University of Washington Libraries, the Seattle Public Library, The Stowe-Day Library, the Schlesinger Library at Radcliffe College, the Library of Congress, the Moorland-Spingarn Research Center at Howard University, The New York Public Library, and The New York Public Library's Schomberg Center for Research in Black Culture. Many of the images in this book were provided by John Leib of J. B. Leib Photography, who searched through his own collection and several archives for photographs of women during the Civil War.

Many people supplied me with research leads and reading lists, for which I am very grateful. Elaine Chang and Bill Lyons generously provided the computer on which this book was written. Christine Laing, Norm Bolotin, Sandi Harner, and Anita Hardy at Laing Communications saw the project through all its phases with their usual dedication and flair.

Thanks to Barry Foy for his careful editing of an early draft of the manuscript, and to Wendy Hamand Venet, Scott Ellsworth, Brian Pohanka, and John and Jaye Zola, who reviewed a later draft and provided invaluable insights and suggestions for improvement. Finally, thanks to my husband, Todd Campbell, for his advice, editing, and encouragement.

Index

Page numbers in *italics* refer to photographs and illustrations

97

Picture Credits

The photographs and illustrations in this book are from the following sources and are used with their permission:

Anacostia Museum, Washington, D.C. • page 91

Boston Public Library • page 46

Chicago Historical Society • pages 22, 30–31

Detroit Public Library (Burton Historical Collection), • page 17

J. B. Leib Photography Co., York, Pa. • pages 8, 15, 18, 24, 37, 50, 52–53, 66–67, 70–71, 72, 82–83

Library of Congress, Washington, D.C. • pages 3, 27, 59, 61, 62, 69, 73, 77, 78, 80, 87, 90

Moorland-Spingarn Research Center, Howard University, Washington, D.C. • pages 4, 74, 76, 89

The Museum of the Confederacy (Eleanor S. Brockenbrough Library), Richmond, Va. • page 21

National Archives, Washington, D.C. • 32, 60

The Schlesinger Library, Radcliffe College, Cambridge, Mass. • page 29

Schomburg Center for Research in Black Culture, The New York Public Library, Astor, Lenox and Tilden Foundations • pages ii, 6–7, 13

State Archives of Michigan, Lansing, Mich. • pages 54, 56

The Stowe-Day Library, Hartford, Conn. • page 9

U.S. Army Military History Institute, Carlisle Barracks, Pa. • pages 23, 35, 38, 42–43, 45, 48, 49, 75, 85

Yale University Art Gallery (Mabel Brady Garvan Collection), New Haven, Conn. • page viii